CREEPY CRAWLY FACT FRENZY!

by Penelope S. Nelson

CAPSTONE PRESS
a capstone imprint

Published by Capstone Press, an imprint of Capstone
1710 Roe Crest Drive, North Mankato, Minnesota 56003
capstonepub.com

Creepy Crawly Fact Frenzy! was originally published as *Totally Amazing Facts About Creepy-Crawlies*, copyright 2018 by Capstone Press.

Copyright © 2026 by Capstone. All rights reserved. No part of this publication may be reproduced in whole or in part, or stored in a retrieval system, or transmitted in any form or by any means, electronic, mechanical, photocopying, recording, or otherwise, without written permission of the publisher.

Library of Congress Cataloging-in-Publication Data is available on the Library of Congress website.

ISBN: 9798875233449 (hardcover)
ISBN: 9798875233395 (paperback)
ISBN: 9798875233401 (ebook PDF)

Summary: Did you know that spiders don't like the smell of peppermint? Or that a dung beetle can carry more than 1,000 times its own weight? Whether you are in the mood to browse or to devour a book in one sitting, dozens of bite-size facts and surprising photos will teach you all sorts of cool things about these creepy crawlies!

Editorial Credits
Editors: Alison Deering and Chris Harbo; Designer: Jaime Willems; Media Researcher: Svetlana Zhurkin; Production Specialist: Whitney Schaefer

Alamy: Nigel Cattlin, 59; Getty Images: Alan Tunnicliffe Photography, 14, FMT Fotografia, 29, Jasius, 51, Jojo Dexter, 36, Kristian Bell, 34, Lukman_M, 37, Oxford Scientific, 24, Santiago mc, 7, Tim Bingham, 40; Minden Pictures: Nature Production/Satoshi Kuribayashi, 33; Shutterstock: Akif Oztoprak, 45, Aleksandr Lazarenko, 9, Alex Stemmer, 54, Andrii Afanasiev, 23, Artush, 25, 32 (bottom), Brian Lasenby, 55, CkyBe (speech bubbles), cover and throughout, Couperfield, 61, Dan Olsen, 57, DMV Photography, 16, Dora Zett, 28, Dr Morley Read, 31 (top), Eric Isselee, 62, ferbthi, 21, gn8 (rays and lines), cover and throughout, Guppic the duck, cover (accessories), I Wayan Sumatika, 63, IanRedding, 8, Idas Dasuki, 56, Iresha Udani, 35, irin-k, cover (wasp, fly, beetle, centipede), JossK, 42, kamnuan, 60, Kenneth Vargas Torres, 39, Kristian Bell, 17, Kurit afshen, back cover, 4 (middle), kurt_G, 43, Littlekidmoment, 18, Lukas Jonaitis, 52, MakroBetz, 1 (top), 13, 58, MasterOfVectors, cover (bug background), Mirko Graul, 12, mistak, 46, narong sutinkham, 19, Nattasak Buranasri, 20, New Africa, 5 (bottom), NuayLub, 30, Oleksii Kriachko, 5 (top), P.F.Mayer, 15, Pavel Krasensky, 27, 41, PetlinDmitry, 50, Pichit Sansupa, 47, 64, Pixel-Shot, cover (tarantula), Protasov AN, 4 (left and right), pryzmat, 22, reptiles4all, 53, Rin Boonprasan, 38, Rod Williams, 1 (bottom), 10, Rosadi adi, 44, Ryan M. Bolton, 49, thirawatana phaisalratana, 48, TinoFotografie, 26, Toeizuza Thailand, cover (ants), Toseef Yousaf (bug silhouettes), 3 and throughout, v_kulieva (gradient background), back cover and throughout, Vinicius R. Souza, 31 (bottom), WildMedia, 32 (top), Yutias, 6, Zeno Swijtink, 11

Any additional websites and resources referenced in this book are not maintained, authorized, or sponsored by Capstone. All product and company names are trademarks™ or registered® trademarks of their respective holders.

Printed and bound in the USA. PO 6307

TABLE OF CONTENTS

A Skin-Crawling Collection
of Creepy Crawly Facts 4

Winged Wonders.. 6

Pesky Pests 18

Crafty Critters 30

Spooky Spine-Tinglers 46

A SKIN-CRAWLING COLLECTION OF CREEPY CRAWLY FACTS

Are you fascinated by bugs, insects, and other tiny critters? Do you want to know ABSOLUTELY EVERYTHING about them? Well, look no further! This book will dish out all sorts of info about dancing bees, headless cockroaches, assassin bugs, and much more. So don't waste another minute! Turn the page for a frenzy of creepy crawly facts!

BRACE YOURSELF! SOME OF THESE CRITTERS MAY GIVE YOU THE SHIVERS!

WINGED WONDERS

Dragonflies have been around for 300 million years!

A dragonfly has two pairs of wings that can beat separately.

Dragonflies can fly 20 miles (32 kilometers) per hour!

Moths get ready to fly by vibrating their wings.

A hummingbird moth's tongue is longer than its whole body!

WOW!

A LUNA MOTH'S TAIL SPINS BEHIND IT AS IT FLIES.

The wing tips of Atlas moths look like snake heads!

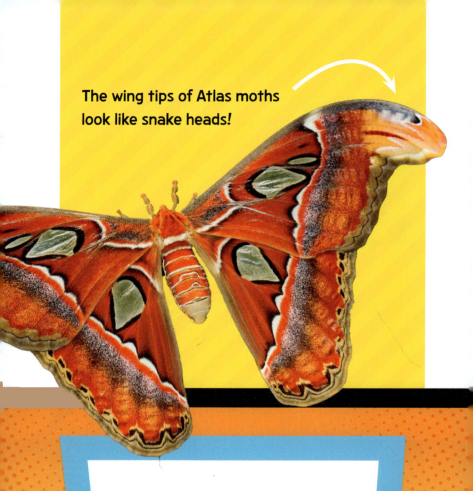

The dead leaf butterfly looks like a dried-up leaf.

The Cramer's 88 butterfly looks like it has the number 88 on its wings.

When a queen bee dies, the worker bees feed young female bee larvae a special food. The food is called royal jelly.

The first fertile bee to hatch will kill the other female bee larvae. She will then become the queen bee.

Bees dance to tell other bees where flowers are located. Scientists call it the "waggle dance."

Wasps can recognize one other's faces.

14

WOW!

A JEWEL WASP STINGS A COCKROACH'S BRAIN. THEN THE WASP TRICKS THE COCKROACH INTO BEING FOOD FOR ITS BABIES.

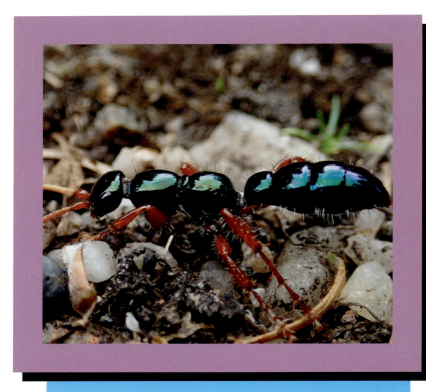

The Australian blue ant isn't really an ant. It's a flower wasp.

Australian blue ants will sting a mole cricket. Then the blue ants lay their eggs inside the cricket.

After hatching, the young blue ants eat the paralyzed cricket!

PESKY PESTS

Head lice attack only humans.

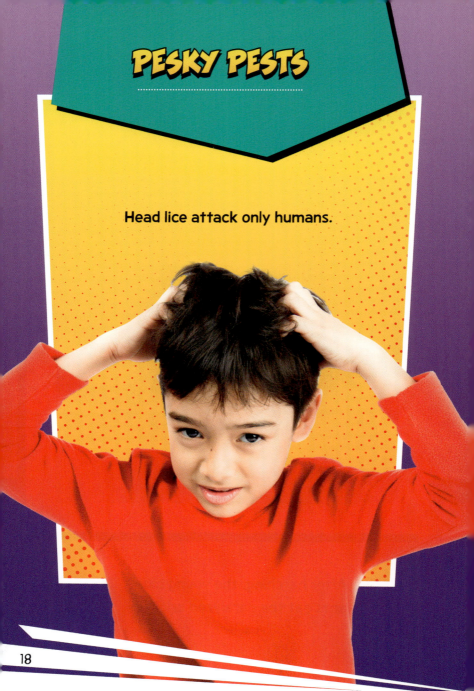

WOW!

ONCE THEY ARE IN HUMAN HAIR, HEAD LICE DRINK BLOOD FROM THE SCALP.

Male cockroaches eat bird poop.

A cockroach can live for a week without its head. It will die only because it can't eat or drink that way.

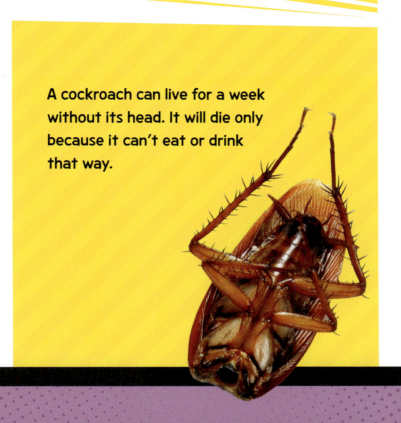

Some cockroaches hatch from eggs inside their mother's body.

A tick can grow to be as big as a marble.

When a tick finds an animal, it inserts a tube into the animal's skin and sucks up blood.

Termites can unearth gold when building their nests.

Termite mounds can be up to 20 feet (6 meters) high!

Termites line their houses with their own poop!

Bed bugs find sleeping humans by sensing the carbon dioxide humans exhale.

A bed bug can attack a person more than 400 times in one night!

Fleas will nest on furry hosts, such as dogs and cats.

WOW!

FLEAS DRINK THE BLOOD OF THEIR HOST!

A female flea can lay up to 50 eggs each day.

CRAFTY CRITTERS

Caterpillars feel touch through the hairs on their bodies.

A saturniid caterpillar's spines can sting attackers.

A giant swallowtail caterpillar looks like bird poop!

Male stag beetles are battle beetles! They have antler-shaped jaws for fighting.

A male giraffe weevil uses its long neck to fight.

Bombardier beetles spray attackers with chemicals. The spray can get as hot as 212 degrees Fahrenheit (100 degrees Celsius)!

If dung beetles didn't exist, most of the ground would be covered in poop!

A dung beetle can carry more than 1,000 times its own weight.

Some researchers think dung beetles may use stars in the night sky as a navigation system.

Some ladybugs have stripes instead of dots.

Sunburst diving beetles can breathe underwater.

A tortoise beetle hides its legs and head under its shell when attacked.

Ants cross gaps in leaves and rocks by using other ants as bridges.

The jaws of a leaf cutter ant vibrate 1,000 times per second!

Leaf cutter ants work together in groups of hundreds or thousands.

Fire ants latch onto one other and swim together to survive during a flood.

Driver ants communicate with their antennae.

Saharan silver ants can live in 120°F (49°C) heat. They use their hair to reflect sunlight and control body temperature.

Assassin bugs are sneaky! They wait and trap their prey.

An assassin bug sucks out its prey's body fluids through a straw-like mouthpart.

An assassin bug uses dead bugs as camouflage. It glues the dead bugs on its back like a suit of armor.

43

Praying mantises usually eat other bugs headfirst.

A praying mantis moves so quickly that the human eye can't see it catch a bug.

WOW!

A FEMALE PRAYING MANTIS SOMETIMES EATS A MALE PRAYING MANTIS.

SPOOKY SPINE-TINGLERS

Even though spiders have eight eyes, some can't see very well.

All spiders make silk, but some don't spin webs.

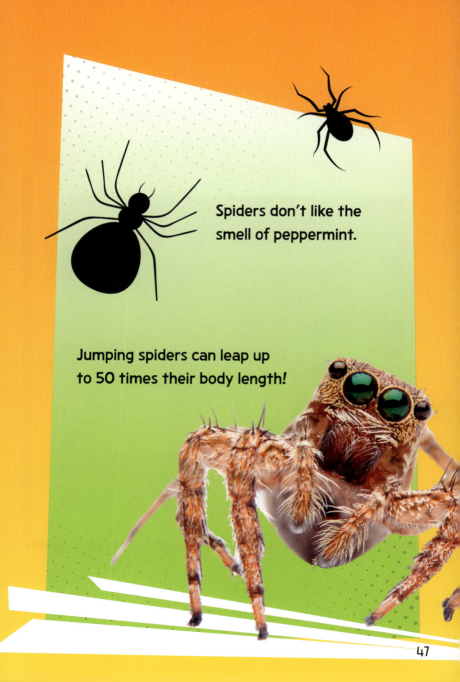

Spiders don't like the smell of peppermint.

Jumping spiders can leap up to 50 times their body length!

Tarantulas live underground.
Their burrows are lined with webs.

A tarantula's large fangs inject venom into prey.

A TARANTULA SUCKS OUT THE INSIDES OF ITS PREY.

49

The Goliath birdeater spider can grow to be 1 foot (30.5 centimeters) long.

The Goliath birdeater spider not only eats birds. It will also eat small mice or lizards!

The Goliath birdeater spider's fangs are nearly 1 inch (2.5 cm) long.

A wolf spider has eight eyes lined up in three rows.

Two of a wolf spider's eyes are near the top of its head.

Wolf spiders lay several dozen eggs at once. The mother will carry the eggs on her back.

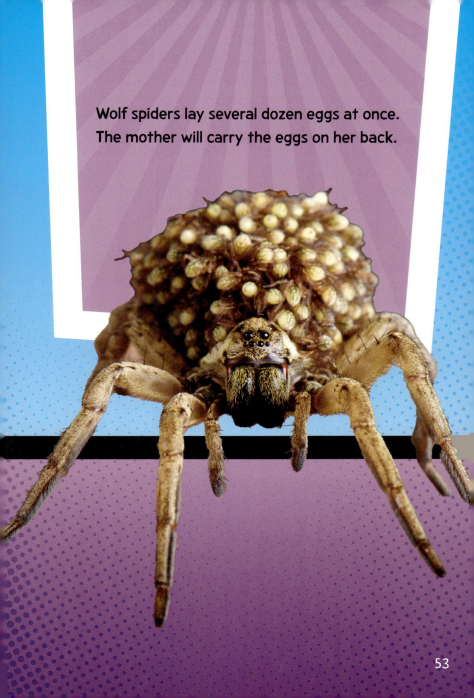

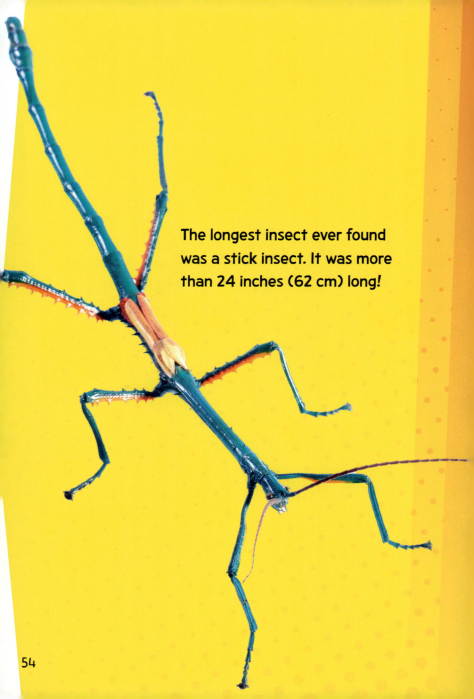

The longest insect ever found was a stick insect. It was more than 24 inches (62 cm) long!

54

Stick insects change their color to match their surroundings.

Centipedes use their poisonous claws to paralyze prey!

Millipedes can have more than 300 pairs of legs.

A slug can have up to 100,000 teeth.

A slug's slime helps it slither smoothly over the ground.

A FEMALE SLUG CAN REPRODUCE WITHOUT A MATE.

Maggots are fly larvae!
They eat rotting meat.

Maggots can help solve crimes.

Scientists study maggots on corpses to determine a time of death.

The biggest scorpion is almost 7 inches (18 cm) long!

Scorpions use their poisonous tails to kill or paralyze prey!

If a mother scorpion can't find enough insects to eat, she will eat her babies.

OTHER BOOKS IN THIS SERIES